children's book of

Family Blessings

WRITTEN BY

Ellen J. Kendig

ILLUSTRATIONS BY

Phyllis V. Saroff

Paulist Press
New York/Mahwah, N.J.

For my children, who are a continual source
of inspiration to me.
—E. J. K.

For Anthony and Daniel.
—P. V. S.

Text copyright © 1999 by Ellen J. Kendig
Illustrations © 1999 by Phyllis V. Saroff

Cover illustration by Phyllis V. Saroff
Cover design by Therese Borchard

Library of Congress Cataloging-in-Publication Data

Kendig, Ellen J.
    Children's book of family blessings / by Ellen J. Kendig ;
illustrations by Phyllis V. Saroff.
        p. cm.
    Summary: A collection of original blessings for family members,
days of the week, special days, and special reasons.
     ISBN 0-8091-6667-4 (alk. paper)
     1. Children Prayer-books and devotions--English. [1. Prayers.]
I. Saroff, Phyllis V., ill.   II. Title.
BV4870.K45 1999
242'.82--dc21

                                              99-38757
                                            CIP

Published by Paulist Press
997 Macarthur Boulevard
Mahwah, New Jersey 07430

www.paulistpress.com

Printed and bound in Mexico

Table of Contents

Praying the Day

Praying the Week

Praying on Special Days

Anniversary Prayer
Birthday Prayer
Prayer on Thanksgiving
Christmas Prayer
Easter Prayer

Praying for Special Reasons

For a Safe Trip
For Someone Sick
For Someone Who Has Died
For a Pet
For Peace
For a Special Challenge
For a Problem

Praying
the Day

FOR MOM

Loving God,
bless my mom
as she goes about her daily tasks,
and cares for our home and family.
Bless her day
and all the work she does.
Bless her hands
and all that she touches.
Bless her heart
and all the people she loves.
Please hold her in your heart
now and forever.
Amen.

PAULIST PRESS

Review Copy

We look forward to receiving your review. Please be sure to send us two copies when it appears. Thank you.

Hugh G. Lally
PAULIST PRESS
997 Macarthur Boulevard,
Mahwah, N.J. 07430
(201) 825-7300

For Dad

Father in Heaven,
thank you for giving me
this father on earth
who is a lot like you.
He takes care of us
and keeps us safe.
He plays with me
and teaches me things.
Bless his work time
and his relaxing time.
And keep him near to you
all day long.
Amen.

FOR MY BROTHER OR SISTER

Dear Jesus,
protect and guide
my brother/sister today,
and keep him/her
in your care always.
I know that you said,
"Whatever you do
to my brother or sister,
you do that to me."
Help us to always get along
and show our love
for each other.
Amen.

FOR MY GRANDPARENTS

Dear God,
I'm really glad
you created grandparents!
They give huge hugs,
terrific treats,
and they're always proud
when you do something great!
I pray that you'll be
with my grandparents today,
protecting them
and guiding them,
because I love them so much.
Amen.

For My Whole Family

Loving Father,
you put me
in this special family
because you knew
they would give me
just the kind of love I need.
Thanks for picking us out
for each other!
Keep us all healthy
and happy
and full of love
for one another.
Amen.

FOR OUR HOME

Good God,
bless our home,
which keeps the rain
off our heads
and the cold out in the winter.
May it always be
strong and sturdy,
comfy and cozy.
Bless our refrigerator and stove,
our bathtub and TV,
and all the other good things
we have.
I know you are everywhere, God.
It's nice to think you are here
in our home with us.
Amen.

Mealtime Prayer

Wonderful God,
fill us with healthy
and delicious food.
Fill us with love
as we enjoy each other's company
and share the events of the day.
Fill us with joy in your presence
here within our family circle.
Fill us with thankfulness
for these and all our blessings.
Amen.

BEDTIME PRAYER

Good night, God!
Thank you for the day that's done.
As I lay my sleepy head
upon my pillow,
I pray that you will cover me
with a blanket of love
and tuck me in with tender care.
May I fall fast asleep
and have peaceful dreams,
safe within your loving arms,
till morning comes again.
Amen.

FOR THE SCHOOL DAY

Holy Spirit,
be with me today in school.
May I listen well
and learn much.
May I work hard
and do my best.
May I grow
in understanding
of myself, others,
and the world
you have created.
Amen.

PLAYTIME PRAYER

Jesus, my Friend,
thank you for playtime blessings:
for jumping and climbing,
hopping and skipping,
whirling, twirling,
hiding, sliding;
for running out of breath
and catching it again;
for playing make-believe
and laughing till my sides hurt;
for toys and games
and sports of all sorts;
and, most of all, for good friends
who are so much fun to play with.
Amen.

Praying
the Week

MONDAY

Father in Heaven,
on Monday you made light
so that the universe
would no longer be in darkness.
Bless us at this bright beginning
of a brand new week.
Help us to make a fresh start
in spreading the light of your love
to everyone we meet.
Amen.

TUESDAY

Loving Creator,
on Tuesday you made the land,
the sky, and the seas.
Thank you for squishy mud pies
and lucky rocks;
for deep blue skies
and clouds in animal shapes;
for grand sand castles
and beautiful beach shells.
Help us to take good care
of planet earth
and all that is on it.
Amen.

WEDNESDAY

Dear Lord,
on Wednesday you made
plants and trees.
Thank you for dandelion bouquets
and clover crowns;
for grass that tickles
the bottoms of bare feet;
for trees to climb
and wood for campfires.
Help us to appreciate
all the plants you have given us,
even broccoli.
Amen.

THURSDAY

God of Wonder,
on Thursday you made
the lights of the heavens.
Thank you for the sun
that chases away the storm
with rainbow-smiles;
for the moon,
our nightlight in the dark;
for shining stars
to make wishes on.
May you be our guiding light
by day and night.
Amen.

FRIDAY

Heavenly Father,
on Friday you made creatures
of the water and sky,
animals that swim
and soar and spout:
sharks and eagles and whales,
goldfish, robins, and roosters.
Bless our family this morning
as we awake
to the songs of the birds
celebrating the end
of a good week.
Amen.

SATURDAY

Our Father,
on Saturday you made
the creatures of the earth,
including humans.
You made us in your image,
which means we are
somehow like you!
May the grace and goodness
you put inside each of us
help us to enjoy each other
and all of your creation today.
Amen.

SUNDAY

Holy God,
on Sunday you rested,
and sat back and felt good
about all you had created.
As we visit
your house today,
may we feel very close
to you and one another.
Bless us as we take time
to relax,
to be with each other,
and to celebrate
all your gifts to us.
Amen.

Praying on
Special Days

ANNIVERSARY

Loving Lord,
today we celebrate the anniversary
of (*name event*),
and all the joy that has come
from that special day.
Help us always to remember
that all good things
come from you,
and to give thanks
for the many blessings
you shower upon us.
Amen.

BIRTHDAY PRAYER

God of Joy,
today we have special treats,
presents, and lots of fun
to celebrate the birthday
of (*name person*).
We thank you for this person's life
and the wonderful gifts he/she
has brought to our lives.
We ask you to bring him/her
extra happiness and love
today and in the coming year.
Amen.

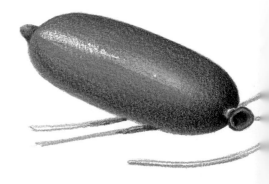

PRAYER ON THANKSGIVING

Thank you, God,
for this feast
and the food you give us every day
(especially pizza);
for our home and family
and the people close to us;
for life and love
and all the things
that make our hearts happy,
especially (*name something*).
Thank you, God!

CHRISTMAS PRAYER

Baby Jesus,
today we celebrate
that day you were born:
a tiny baby who would grow up
to be the Savior of the world.
As we share love and presents,
help us to remember that you were
the first and best
Christmas gift ever:
the Father's gift of love
to the world.
Happy Birthday!

EASTER PRAYER

Risen Lord,
you rose from the dead
to bring us life forever.
May the beauty of springtime
and the colored eggs,
marshmallow chickies,
and chocolate bunnies
that we find in our Easter baskets
remind us to celebrate
our new life in you.
Alleluia!

Praying for Special Reasons

FOR A SAFE TRIP

Lord and Guide,
be with our family
as we set out on this trip.
We thank you for the fun
we will have
as we see new sights
and share new adventures.
Help us to stay on the right path,
and keep us safe
from any danger.
Amen.

For Someone Sick

Jesus, Divine Healer,
I pray today for (*name person*),
who is sick.
Just as you worked miracles
and healed people in the Bible,
please lay your hands
upon him/her.
Touch him/her with
your strength, love,
and healing power,
so that he/she
may get well soon.
Amen.

For Someone Who Has Died

Loving Father,
I pray today for all
who have died,
especially for (*name person*),
whom I love very much.
I believe that he/she
is with you now in heaven,
safe within your loving arms,
and that one day,
I will see him/her there.
Until then, I ask you
to hug him/her close
to your heart.
Amen.

For a Pet

God of All Creatures,
you made animals
to be our friends and companions.
I pray this day
for furry, fuzzy, feathery pets
and slippery, slimy, slithery ones,
especially for my pet, (*name pet*).
Help me take good care
of him/her.
Watch over him/her
and keep him/her healthy
and safe from harm.
Amen.

FOR PEACE

Jesus, Prince of Peace,
when we have disagreements,
help us to settle them
peacefully.
When we are angry,
help us to talk it out.
When feelings are hurt,
help us to say we're sorry
and to forgive.
Bless our hearts and our world
with the gift of your peace.
Amen.

For a Special Challenge

Dear God,
I have a big challenge
ahead of me today.
Help me use the special talents
you have given me
to succeed.
Give me the strength
to try my hardest.
And let me remember that,
win or lose,
you will always love me.
Amen.

For a Problem

God of Mercy,
I have a problem
that is making me feel upset.
Please give me the courage I need
to handle this problem
and the faith to know
everything will work out
according to your plan.
I give this problem to you,
trusting that your heart
holds all my cares.
Amen.